Unsung Verses
Haimnauth Ramkirath

Copyright © 2021 Haimnauth Ramkirath

All rights reserved. No part of this book may be reproduced or transmitted in any form or by any means, electronic or mechanical, including photocopying, recording or by any information storage and retrieval system without permission in writing from the publisher.

New Sunrise Press—Bayonne, NJ
ISBN: 978-1-7363733-0-9
Library of Congress Control Number: 2020925570
Title: *Unsung Verses*
Author: Haimnauth Ramkirath
Digital distribution | 2021
Paperback| 2021

Published in the United States by New Book Authors Publishing.

Dedication

This book is dedicated to my late parents, my mother, Nanki and my Father, Ramkirath. Their lives exemplified the simplicity and beauty in this collection of poetry.

Just living is not enough….
one must have sunshine,
freedom,
and a little flower.

—Hans Christian Anderson

Table of Contents

Author's Note vii
He Planted A Tree 1
Sunset 2
The Lotus Rises 3
The River Rushes On 5
Little Butterfly 6
If I Can 7
When We Cease to Smile 9
Waiting for The Train 10
A Brighter Morn 12
The Strings of the Sitar 14
A Gardenia 15
The Kite 16
The Flame 18
Here's A Friend 20
The Lake 22
The Poem Speaks 23
Blanket of Charm 25
A Line Above the Waters 26
A Fallen City 27
The Spirit of the Oak Tree 28
Tattered Sail 29
The Flute 30
Awaken by Songs 31

Before We Know	32
A Walk	33
Autumn	34
Glimpses of Nature	35
The Perfume of the Water Lily	37
Time	38
Songs of Hope	40
He's Not There	42
A Bricklayer	44
Uncharted Waters	45
The Blazing Chariot	47
A Million Lights	48
My Childhood Days	49
The Deep Open Sea	51
Some Unfinished Work	52
What Manner of Hand	53
Invisible	55
Don't Give Up on the World	57
Unseen they Roam	58
Unknown	60
Life is Better on the Porch	62
A Host of Stars Bright	63
A Different World, A Different Feeling	64
Patterns	65
Spinning Wheels	67
Blighted Flowers	68
The Mango Tree	69
Breath of an Uneasy Wind	71
The Masks	72
Miracles	74
Gorges	75

Memories of the Ocean	76
Every Throbbing Heart	78
It Watches in Silence	79
My Garden of Flowers	81
A Wretched Wind	82
The Threads Interwoven	84
Look at Nature	86
Oak Trees and Reeds	88
Dark Depths of the Sea	90
Heart of a Child	91
Butterfly on My Shoulder	94
A Felt Exultation	95
The Love of a Mother	96
A High Call	98
One Day at a Time	99
A Cable of Steel	100
Restless Longing	102
Numbers	103
My Ancestors	105
A Virus	107
A Serpentine Foe	108
A Dream	110
How Long?	112
I Feel the Pain	114
Three Rivers	115
Music	116
How We Treat Our Feathered Friends	117
Condos & High-Rises	118
Lift Your Mind	120
Cosmic Travelers	121
That Dreaded Classroom	122

Far-Off Places	123
Like the Space Unscathed	124
Rising from the Ashes	126
A Gentle Whisper	127
Dawn	128
A Ship	130
A Smile & A Song	131
Waiting for Spring	132
A Song, A Poem, A Dance	134
Heart, Flesh & Bones	135
That's the Place	136
The Mirror	137
That's When	138
If We Could	139
Oh! Little Canary	142
About the Author	144

Author's Note

In line with my three previously published works of poetry, this collection primarily focuses on the beauty and the rhythms of the natural world. It also deals with the related themes of hope, illumination, fear, joy, harmony, and much more, and all through the sounds and sights of natural, meditative images. My intention is to present pictures and images of the natural world that will touch the hearts of both the young and the old, and inspire them to appreciate, even for a passing moment, the ever-changing beauty, and the ravishing delights of the world around us.

Our fair world is saturated with breaking news and images that reveal the darker sides of human nature and experiences. Now more than ever we need strength, inspiration, and hope. We need to make meaning from our hectic lives, and to face the challenges ahead with an inner resilience and poise. The terrible scourge of the covid-19 virus has greatly tempered our natural exuberance. The resultant feelings of hopelessness, fear, anger, pessimism, and depression are widespread and palpable. This collection aims to lift the mind, and to offer a solace that is immediately refreshing and almost tranquilizing. Some of the poems in this collection deal with the pains and the horrors of covid-19, and the unspeakable tragedy it brought to our world. There is the perennial voice of hope and expectation that our humanity and ingenuity with ultimately triumph over this vicious enemy, but there is also the anguish. As a poet and a sensitive human being, I cannot help but ask:

How long the silence of festive drums,
the caution to embrace a cherished friend?

The writing style is simple, natural, and fluid. This is a thoughtful compilation with the focus on the crafting of the poems and using the various poetic devices and imagery to present the language that most closely and clearly reflects the theme, emotion, or inspiration. I have tried to reflect an innate simplicity and sincerity in each poem. I hope that this collection of poems will touch the heart of every reader.

He Planted A Tree

The old man planted a tree in the park,
in the shadow of a red oak tall.
When stormy winds shook it hard,
sheltered it within the portals of his heart.
But the old man died before the tree grew tall.

He never took a little rest under its shade.
He never saw the nest the robin made,
or in fall its leaves of flaming yellow and crimson red.
Never saw the tiger moth butterfly on its leaf alight,
or squirrels mount its trunk in blithe delight.

Never a witness to its impassive strength—
resolute in the fiery blast of the sun's wrath,
unrattled by storms and lightning strikes.
But the old man knew these things all along.
He would never see the tree tall and strong.

That's why he planted it with a song
that his spirit may live on
in that which is suckled to the earth,
and for you and me and the world to see—
beauty of life that's in a tree.

Sunset

I gazed at the sun gradually sinking
into the bosom of the deep sea.
A fading lamp,
but a thousand delights
time compressed,
and in a span of moments—
a blaze of the firmament.

A parting gift—
a bed of crimson red
the sun makes to rest.
The embrace, the dance of color and light,
like the distant glow of a forest alight.
Autumn leaves strewn in the sky,
infinite hues subdued and bright
streaming through scattered fabrics of clouds.

Compelled to gaze long
until that lamp was gone.
Still ten thousand shades of vanishing light.
Deep meditative silence fell on the land.
Then—
the majestic curtain abruptly closed:
darkness swallows every trace of its eternal foe.

The Lotus Rises

Deep roots in muddy, slimy pond,
but like the elephant, unyielding and strong,
the lotus heeds the call of dawn.
Rises from depths languid and murky,
and like pure waters of a gushing spring,
bursts into profuse blooms of perfume
above the turgid surface of a weary pond.

Untainted by mud, lifts its face
like sprays from a cascade.
When a mild wind stirs the silence,
it dances with an unearthly radiance—
homage to the chariot mounting the horizon.
Water droplets precariously slide on its leaf,
like one standing on the edge of a cliff,
like these fragile threads of our breath.

Its story, a never-ending odyssey.
Dark depths of despair to illumination.
Cuts drowsy waters of loathsome desires,
awakens with the fire of a soul inspired—
the human journey in a flower captured.

Closes petals at night and sinks under,
and when night dies in day's soft embrace,
quiet miracle on the pond displays.

In the stillness of deep awakening chants,
rises immaculately with blooms defiant,
as the human heart opens and reveals
in resplendent colors—
a thousand-petalled lotus.

The River Rushes On

Boulder-ridden miles, narrow suffocated passes,
a thousand tumbles, a thousand pains,
but the river searches for the sea again.

Cliffs, mountains, scenic vales, and plains,
a thousand charms, a thousand delights,
the river meanders, tarries a while.

Would rather live here in the tranquil pure air,
but there's a resolve in its currents strong
to seek the sea where it belongs.

And with an impetuous urge and rush
moves with wings for time ill spent—
to lose itself in the greater swell of the sea.

Consummation of a journey of trickling drops
of water, then torrents, rapids, and violent surges—
a power unflinching in its restless primordial desire.

Little Butterfly

Like dew on the tip of a reed,
a little butterfly alights on a peach tree—
an unobtrusive visitor as could ever be.
Light like a flake of snow—
what sweet burden a leaf to show.

I hesitate to touch its wings
lest I besmirch fragile fabrics weaved—
Autumn's colors sprinkled on orchid's petals.
And our needlework of glittering threads
ill compared to these silken wings of crimson gold.

The little butterfly in a dreamlike stillness.
A blithe thing at rest,
as the leaf trembles in the wind's breath.
But was born with wings and glamor
to cut the air in sunlight and passing showers.

Lifts from the leaf with breathtaking ease,
like a gem studded with angelic wings.
A quick dash to a tree or climbing vine.
Another leaf or flower to feel its tinseled touch,
and adorned with the imprint of unearthly dust.

If I can…

If I can wrap a trembling robin in my palms.
Send a caged canary over mountains and sea.
Prop a newborn tree with the strings of my heart
as I watch it rises in the morn, in the twilight's charm.

If I can wipe the tears of a distraught brother.
Comfort a forsaken heart-broken mother.
Remove a splintered wood from a child's path,
and watch my own trail as the clouds loom dark.

If I can in feeling and compassion
be like dark rain-borne clouds over cracked earth.
Ready to nourish minds and bodies
along winding vales and stretches of vines.

If I can remove the dust on the mirror of my heart
to see the light resplendent in all.
Resolute along the path long and weary,
as the sun hides its face, the day grows dreary,

If I can listen to the tales of an old rover of the seas,
but fashion my adventures and exploits too.
And when the day closes with a flood of nostalgia
dream of pretty maidens and isles of corals.

If I can turn the dusty pages of books,

but know the rapture in babbling brooks, wild woods.
The silence of the embrace of day and night.
The setting sun in the dance of color and light.

If I can still trace the falcon's path
when back and joints seldom hide their wrath,
and smile with a song in the heart
when the stars beckon me to depart.

When We Cease to Smile

Deep cuts and bruises on its trunk.
Its limbs tormented and wounded,
but the tree waves and smiles at every passerby.
The fields of corn, the grassy plains
smile in sun and rains,
and the trampled dust
smile at every wind that picks them up.

When we cease to smile,
no warmth on faces, no sparkle in eyes.
We need to listen to the sweet refrain
of the timeless song along the tranquil shore.
The soft footfalls, the laughter of little children
whose smiles clothe the hour
with the freshness of spring flowers.
We need to watch the stars
that send glad tidings to the night.
The ocean that swells with stories to tell,
and a hummingbird that hovers and flaps it wings
faster than eyes can wink.

Waiting for The Train

I am in a boiling cauldron—
a sweltering subway station.
Music blaring, drums thundering
over frenzied rushing and shouting.
Scents of cologne and exotic perfume
commingling with the reek
a stingy stagnant air brings,
and waiting, waiting, and waiting.

Watching over-sized rats
running near tracks and disappearing.
Broken tiles, crawling disfiguring stains,
graffiti, dust, and debris that remain.
The homeless sleeping and dreaming.
Lovers embracing and kissing,
and a woman with the fervor of a believer
calling all to repent and surrender.

Weariness written on anxious faces
huddling close to the platform's edge.
Looking, looking, and looking
for that flashlight glowing
out of that dark deep corridor.
When it flickers beams on metal rails,
like crocodile's eyes on a prey,
there's a sudden rush of wind,

and excited faces stepping to greet
the beast rushing and rumbling,
sparks of fire flying, smell of burning,
streaking steel slowing to a screeching stop.
People rushing for air, cool and refreshing:
there's joy in every waiting.

A Brighter Morn

Crushed in the mantle of the earth.
Hardened in the crucible of unrelenting fire.
The carbon never the same each hour—
dies to every dross, every unwanted desire:
a diamond born in a burst of splendor.

And like carbon in its primordial travail,
each day a thousand walls and fences I climb.
Each day I die a thousand times.

Every veil of illusion lifted
every dark vile habit deceived
every tortured pattern of thought unweaved
every fear vanquished by an inward gaze
every citadel of ignorance ablaze
every doubt perished in the blinding sun
every stagnant stream made to run—
untrammeled by the ensnared old that's gone,
like the snake that sheds its skin along—
new pathways beckon me on:
I die to live with a sweeter smile and song.

And when I drop this mortal coil,
never again to trace the falcon's path,
or gaze in the old churchyard—

I will not die.
With a ruddy cheek,
new frontiers I will seek.
New hills, new pastures I will roam.
Fresh fields to furrow on a brighter morn.

The Strings of the Sitar

The strings of the sitar have awakened
with mystical sounds of snow-capped mountains,
rhythms of enchanted gardens, lakes, and streams—
stuff of meditation, songs, sleep, and dreams.

The twang of rolling waves of halcyon days,
surging memories those strings awake.
They rest by a stream with a lively face,
like water gurgling from the mouth of a vase.

They rush with heavy rains as in a monsoon
angry winds, thunder, strikes of lightning
waves crashing
rivers bursting their banks.

Then soothing rhythms of the sun sinking.
Wings of a condor flapping over the mountain.
The rustling of leaves in a forest deep,
and sounds of the universe stretched to light-years.

A Gardenia

In a lone pot besides a window,
the bud of a gardenia
rises above glossy dark-green leaves.
Opens like a delicate seashell—
velvet soft flowers where beauty dwells.

Like an elephant's tusk
the color of the blooms.
An exotic perfume
floods the living room.
Settles deep onto the soul,
and sends to sleep fragrances on rugs,
bottled scents in outlets snugged.

The gardenia besides the window,
the purity of the Himalayan snow.
Behold the clarity of the petals—
a fitting canvas our dreams to write.

It speaks the language of love.
Awkward for human tongues to utter.
Bedecked in elegance and beauty,
rests on a garland made for eternity,
and the world adores with longing eyes—
a bouquet in which a gardenia smiles.

The Kite

The mounted kite danced and sang,
but not with the freedom of the falcon
tied to no human hand.
It ascended higher and higher,
kissed the clouds,
then in loops of effervescent delight
brushed its tail against the lush earth.

Never such charm and glee
in tinseled paper, thin slices of the conifer tree,
cherry gum, and bamboo skin.
When the wind held its breath,
it gazed with a steady face,
like an ornament held high,
a blithe ribbon blazoned against the sky.

A cue from the wind,
the kite brushed aside worldly decorum.
Danced with a lusty abandon,
and with such daring spirit
that courted high razor-wire fences,
power lines stretched for miles,
and boisterous sprawling trenches.

It dashed against a tall pear tree.
The branches caught its fearless spirit.

They muzzled its song.
Drained its heart of every dance.
Alas! so wretched, so forlorn!
Must be sad for a thing so free
to be stuck on a tree.

The Flame

The flame is bright and steady.
My little earthen lamp of clay.
It rises with a radiance
the sun splashes sea and land,
and with a thousand smiles—
an untroubled face of no earthly wiles.

A faint stream of dark smoke
runs from the brilliance on its face.
The darkness of a thousand years
obliterated by its searching rays.
Oh! how my heart bleeds as it flickers and dies
when a cruel, cold, blustery wind passes by.

But when a gentle wind embraces it with a soft kiss,
it dances with an unearthly bliss.
Then with a stillness—
reveals the red on the robin's breast,
the bright yellow of the kiskadee's plumage,
and the majestic blue of the sky unclouded.

It burns the dross of metals and things,
and which to the human heart clings.
When it's kindled deep within,
ten thousand brighter worlds seen.
And when it stretches to reach the ceiling—

it's the untold joy of an awakening.

Here's A Friend

You shout at him.
He seems a little ashamed,
but scarcely rebels or complains.
If only he could know your every whim.
He would swim the seven seas,
fight with the sun and the wind,
to show what a friend you have in him.

Whether you are up or down,
he's your loyal friend around.
Ready to warm your heart
from the bite of an artic blast.
What sting in these lonely days?
He's here to lift your mood
when the sun is gone.
Listen to your groans, your pains
when the blood slows in veins.

He waits at the door for a hug, a kiss.
Not for the world a sweet embrace to miss.
He seems to know when your spirit is light or heavy,
when he should sit in quiet or just be jolly.
He is ready to share your daily walks
with fun and games at the park—
running for the ball or the limb of a tree,
ever so free when he's with you.

He brings the daily news,
milk bottle and the food.
He keeps a vigil all night
to divert encroaching evil eyes.
When in country or town,
he looks at every corner, every turn
that you may gaze at the full moon
with a friend who wouldn't mind
it's too late to be out in the open.

Friends may leave when you're down,
but here is one who will stick around.
When the light goes out,
he will be your sure guide.
When you are gone from this good earth,
he will wait at the door for a hug, a kiss.
And his love for a human being—
will straddle the majestic firmament.

The Lake

The lake today—
the tranquil mind of a sage.
No ceaseless waves of desire,
no ripples of discontent,
not even a gentle stir of unease
to mark a ruffle on its face.

A mysterious silence it holds.
Even the footfall of a child—
a clap of thunder to its sweet repose.
Like a rare painting on a canvas seen,
beyond the maze of words and meaning:
the lake rests on the lap of eternity.

The lake today
in deep sleep.
Yet fully awake—
greeting the dawn,
saluting the sun:
with peace profound.

The Poem Speaks

I am a poem.
I am made up of words
that run along the page,
and that's why you know
I have more than words to show.
But they are my blood, bones, and flesh,
muscles and sinews deep in my breast.

When they move and flow like a restless river,
my heart beats with rhythms of wonder.
And like the river there is such joy
if you just watch how I flow and meander,
but in the depths of my streams—
pearls and gems never seen.

I scan earth, sky, and heaven
to reveal what's all around.
I say things you have heard a million times,
but in a way to set a fire on your mind.

I carry you on my wings over mountains and seas,
and into the very eye of the dreaded storm,
then for you to rest along the placid deep lake.
I am the voice of a child and that of an old man
who has seen the sun on grassy plains and in the wild.

I fetch a bundle of images, sights, sounds, and color.
I just want you to get the picture,
and when I talk of a sunflower—
it's the universe you should ponder.

Blanket of Charm

Veil of day lifted.
Neon lights of sprawling city,
on giant screen a girl in bikini—
all swallowed by a blinding torch.
Its searching rays
beyond the falcon's gaze,
over land, hills, mountains, and seas.
Awakening humpback whale
and snail, jaguar, and short-tailed quail.

A mild wind sedately enchants.
Daffodils smile and dance,
sweet embrace of morning's warmth.
Streams flow with rhythms of ease.
The rustle of leaves, waves of tall grasses,
music of robin blends with buzz of bees.
The strings of nature's guitar, near and afar,
and hard for the heart to be forlorn—
all wrapped in a blanket of charm.

A Line Above the Waters

I saw a bird skimmed over the river.
Steady like a fleet-footed impala,
it drew a line above the waters,
fine as an unerring arrow.

I held my breath.
The thrill in my breast,
magic, power, and symmetry in wings outstretched.
Yet! wonder of motion at rest.

It gathered speed over deeper restless waters.
Kept pace with it for miles
until it became an ethereal thing
moving to a resplendent shore.

Seen many of its kind,
but none so exquisite, so sublime.
And it raced to my mind,
when I ride waters dark and choppy,
to think of that bird of peerless grace and agility.
But now I must wait with eyes keen.
If fortune favors with a visit again,
may it kiss the waters in a majestic swoop.
I wish to pay homage to that blithe spirit—
that touched a chord deep in my heart.

A Fallen City

If you live to the age of the cedars of Lebanon—
count not your muscles and limbs to be as strong,
or your beauty to linger long
as the trees that built the Temple of Solomon,
buttressed ancient ships from storms,
and whose fragrance rises in the valley of Bsharri.

Behold what time has dealt a city
once obdurate, proud, and unassailable.
Intricate networks of citadels,
slowly cracked, crumbled, and broken.
The enemies virulent and relentless—
cruel intent in marrow and sinews entrenched.

The body of youth like a garden of spring,
gushes with songs, perfume, and charm.
But never a thing has the years more harassed,
this shell we embrace as seasons pass.
And when there's time to anoint the days with songs:
the body can scarce stand another dance.

The Spirit of the Oak Tree

In the woods deep,
I sat beside an old oak tree.
I heard echoes of lamentations of the people.
My head sank on my knees.
My cries awoke the oak tree.
Then it softly whispered to me:
"Do not trouble my shade with your tears
lest they fall on my roots,
and bring blight on my bark
in the day and when it's dark.
We do not lament
when the sun scorches our limbs,
rains and winds lash with bitter stings,
lightning strikes in the cover of night,
and we bleed from humans' insolent might.
When the cruel wind brings us down
to bite the dust on the ground—
we remember we once stood tall in the sun.
But now we embrace Mother Earth at last—
smile as our spirits move fast."

Tattered Sail

You mingle with the crowd in the bar,
and along the city's streets and thoroughfares.
You dance as the music blares.
Seem to be without a worldly care.
But when alone in your rocking chair,
what tortured hours you bear,
what haunts you deep in your being—
the world can but scarcely dream.

You're a stranger to your best of friends,
though together fences you mend.
You're the life of the party.
You laugh, you're so dainty.
Many reckon you the most cheerful girl in town—
if they know the inner wounds you have bound.
And as days and nights roll:
you remain a tattered sail to no wind unfurled.

The Flute

Your hallowed being not stained by human vanity.
Plucked from the limb of a dense bamboo canopy.
Born to make light the burden of care.
Bring on earth the music of celestial spheres.
They massage you with scented oil.
Soothe your skin and joints
with a coat of lacquer and turpentine.
Inscribe designs, engrave precious stones,
and fashion eyes on your face—
you wake up with a lovely gaze.

You feel the soft embrace of the wind.
The sun enters the depths of your being.
You remain mute to their entreaties.
But when the human lips softly caress you,
every fiber rises with music so free
that floods land and sea.
The cobra raises its head, sways in a trance.
Planets and stars in glee dance,
and the human ears can scarce contain
a fountain of ecstatic melodic strains.

Awaken by Songs

No sound of human or machine,
no alarm rudely shattered my dream
of distant isles, placid seas, and coral reefs,
blissful rest under the shade of palm trees.
I awoke to the sounds of orange-breasted robins.
Sweet music rippled from the top of the tree
that guards my window with its sprawling reach.

They seem to have a magical cue
when the golden threads of my dream would end,
and then and only then sweet melodies to send.
Stirring notes after the mystical calm of dawn.
Oh! what sweet respite to the ears,
and to a weary mind—
sunshine to the mist of worldly cares.

No greater joy my day to start,
chorus of robins within the ramparts of my heart.
What rousing songs from my feathered friends
to blunt the fears the day may send.
I long to gaze at their frolic and fun,
but I must make worthy my tongue—
songs of praise for the effulgent sun.

Before We Know

The seconds, minutes, and hours pass.
The days never long last,
like mist that fades in the sun's blast,
and before we know
we grow whiskers white as snow.

Seasons of mirth tarry for a while.
But as the sun ripens wine-filled grapes,
and the robin sings loud for a mate,
winter's wretched steps steal a march,
send to sleep our blithe days—
the garden of green withers,
our bodies grow distempered.

Reckon not the years to still be there.
They have work elsewhere.
As we sow and reap, cry and sing,
they move as if with wings.
And when our hours, days, and years are done:
have we measure their width and breath,
and plumbed their depths
with works of selfless service and love?

A Walk

A walk is not the beads of sweat on the forehead.
The calories and miles burned.
Blood shooting through the veins.
Joints and muscles that pain.
Not the blisters on toes.
The battered boots you show.

A walk is a rousing, a rebound
when your spirits are down.
Greeting the new barber in town.
Seeing the flowers of spring around.
Trees you have seen ten thousand times—
yet to see in a burst of glory in the NOW.

A walk is watching gulls diving in the sea.
Squirrels mounting tree trunks with glee.
Touching soft wet green grass,
and slippery rocks covered with moss.
To hum a tune in the park,
and watch the stars when it grows dark.

A walk is keeping with the rhythms
of rivers and seas, the air that moves so free.
To see the changing faces of the clouds,
the geese lumbering about.
To behold the charm and the magic
in silent streams, and restless rapids.

Autumn

Autumn is the season to admonish.
Takes from the day when we love to play,
as the sun in haste rides away.
A little sweat we break,
creeping shadows come to say—
wings of night fast on their way.

Seems like yesterday they adorned the trees.
The rustle that brings cherished memories.
Full of life and zest, green and sheen,
proof against rains and raging winds,
but now their sinews drained, and like fragile wings
fall at the slightest whisper of Autumn's wind.

With cunning zeal Autumn marches on.
Sparrows and canaries cease to sing along.
The frost that Autumn brings caresses
chrysanthemums with a deadly sting.
And a mighty shame to disrobe the trees—
send our feathered friends to cross stormy seas.

Glimpses of Nature

The cheetah lazily resting in the savannah,
but in a moment—
a machine super charged:
lean elegant express train on the grassy plain.

Anaconda sleeping in the shallow muddy waters.
Overblown tube that meanders like a river.
Glazed with dark olive green and yellow
round brown blotches and a dark stripe.
In its jaws the power of a lock no key can open,
and in the vise of its coiled embrace,
a gruesome garland of a slow agonizing death.

Nature rises in the giant sequoias.
Their heads adorned with clouds.
Loins draped in fabric thick,
raging flames leave unscathed.
Their eyes have seen Pharaohs,
ancient cities, Harappa and Mohenjo Daro,
walls of Mesopotamia,
Library of Alexandria.

Call of Kilimanjaro—
Africa's breathtaking gift.
Head crowned with ice,
spine carved with hard desert rocks,

and entwined with mosses and ferns.
Lower limbs drenched in tropical heat,
rainfall, lush rain forests deep
where elephants in the wild roam,
and monkeys open a way
through a canopy of banana leaves.

Nature reaches a crescendo—
in Niagara
where the mighty river takes a fall
from a table of rocks high—
ten thousand horses galloping down the track,
reaching the homestretch in a mighty splash,
mouths foaming:
disappearing in the misty blue.

The Perfume of the Water Lily

The perfume of the giant water lily
rises above shallow waters of the Amazon.
Reaches no thoroughfares of humans—
yet is not wasted.

Its aroma lingers in tracks of capybaras.
Sits on branches where toucans gather,
and scarce desires toxic air of towns and cities,
beaten paths of cruel wretched faces.

The perfume of the giant water lily,
like the cloud-drenched peaks of the Pyrenees,
in self-contented bliss rests,
and cares little if the world be impressed—
a gift so swell to the forest.

It rises at the wind's behest,
like frankincense in the temple,
over insects and frogs in forest dark—
as waters of the Amazon rise and fall.

Time

Time like a falcon flies.
When the heart is light; sun shines bright,
cork pops from a bottle of wine,
and music rises above tangled voices.
Time like a choked drain.
When the heart is heavy, clouds dreary,
and every tree that rustles in the wind,
awakens pangs of dark memories.
Time like a far-flung river,
meanders, bring hearts together,
thwarts our cherished desires.

Time mounts the chariot of the sun.
Ripens the corn, stretches the vine,
heals wounds of body and mind.
Listens to the song of the nightingale,
gazes as a seagull kisses the lake,
and a hummingbird like a flying jewel
alights on a cluster of spider flowers.
But for the work it must do
would rather tarry for a while,
and rests besides the tranquil sea
under the shade of a coconut tree.

Time pierces the heart with thorns,
or brings a bouquet of flowers each morn.

Time gathers the storm clouds,
or sends a mild wind to kiss our brows.
Time beckons when to furrow deep in the field,
gather and share the yield.
When to shout with the crowd and tribe.
When in the tranquil waters of the lake to dive.

Songs of Hope

Subdued in the darkness of earth,
but the tiny seed silently sings
a song of hope.
It will be a giant oak.
Will rise like a column,
stretch its limbs in the sun,
and the world will scarce know
it came from a tiny seed in the ground.

A canary captive in a cage.
Pacing back and forth—
what meager room to spread its wings.
What stifling, paltry air to breathe.
And when it should be flying miles
so alone!
in a prison, an exile dark
forged by human hands and hearts.

Forced to defy its captivity
with a song of hope
that a human hand will let it fly
to woods it needs to live and die.
Fashion a cup-shaped nest on a tree,
sit on a cliff, radiant and free,
show a full plumage to a mate,
and never again bound in a cage.

A lone prisoner in a cell deep,
the sun's rays never reach.
Feet in rings of steel.
A piece of cloth over concrete for bed—
incarceration that defiles the vigor of youth.
His gaze barred by high walls of hate.
The only human face he sees:
a guard who pushes into a slot
a bowl of rotten meat and putrid rice.

Each day a painful reminder,
darkness that grows each hour,
and the rage in his heart
searing to tear his mind apart.
But at the pale light of dawn
he hears a song in the branches,
and then the faint roll of drums—
the call of freedom,
and a song of hope in his heart rises.

He's Not There

The fallen mortal coil:
a candle gone bereft of oil,
a wearied tattered coat dropped,
a battered cage—
the bird has flown and gone,
and your river of tears can never reach—
realm of another time and space beyond the seas.

He's not there.
Look not for him in the pitch darkness of night.
Who courted, danced, and dined,
popped a cork from a bottle of wine.
Who sang sweet melodies of faded memories.
Plucked the weeds, furrowed the field of his mind,
and drew the circle of his compassion
beyond the boundary of the roving wind and tide.

He's not there.
Look not for him in far-flung corners of dreams.
Who shared his bread with a homeless man.
Listened to the refrain of his sad song.
Who cleaned the shore of human stench and neglect,
and planted trees for sparrows to build their nests.
Who walked miles to befriend a distraught brother,
and gave to the poor corn from fields he labored.

He's not there
in the cold sepulchered ground.
He is in a house matchless in beauty and light.
He rushes with the tides, runs with the moon,
blooms with buttercups, dances with berries.
And when the heavens light up at night—
he's among the brightest stars.

A Bricklayer

Like the Taj Mahal's gleaming marble of love,
there's beauty and symmetry in my work.
I lay foundations for skyscrapers to shine,
and mighty garrisons to thwart the enemy's line.
In many a sprawling city and town
I rest cobbled stones for folks to walk, horses to trot,
and set cornerstones that speak of deeds renown.

I cover the flesh of humble and stately homes,
weave magic patterns with bricks, marble, and stones.
And when I place the mortar to seal their fate,
kiss and tightly embrace—
they bond with a love so strong,
takes a speeding iron ball,
to break their bones and make them fall.

Uncharted Waters

Each day some uncharted waters.
Each day the sun sports a different face.
The wind wakes with a new rhythm.
The mountain tells another story,
and the water that reaches the knees
not the same when we stepped into the sea.

They roll, sail, dance, and fly,
bring the bountiful rains,
but the way clouds look and stretch
change with the walk of a few steps.
And it's never the same coat of blue—
that splashes that awesome dome each day.

The mirror sees a different body each day.
Every strand of hair a new look.
The blood that coursed through the veins yesterday,
not the same that cries for food today.
The eyes that tracked the falcon's path yesterday,
not the same that strained through the fog today.

The mind with a light or heavy heart,
not a settled bundle of joys or sorrows each day.
The bustling market in the city's square,
a fresh beat and tempo each day,
and the stars that warm our hearts—

never changeless each night we search.

The Blazing Chariot

The tall days of summer around—
ice cream, sand, and sun-drenched fun.
It's an early hour; folks still dreaming,
but the effulgent orb climbing.
Peeping through the dark curtains,
beckoning to behold the mountains.
Summits drenched in molten gold,
like the streets of El Dorado of old.

A far ride that chariot blazoning the sky
as tides come and go, friends bid goodbye.
The wine-filled grapes welcome the exhausted day.
It's just the start of fair May.
The buttercups and lilies don their best dresses.
The vines emboldened to longer stretches,
and when the boy gathers the cows for the day:
the chariot still blazing away.

A Million Lights

I stood at the river's edge
among wildflowers and sculptured rocks.
A flock of geese lumbered on grass.
The sun was almost overhead.
Clouds hang like feathers of the egret.
Like stars at night so bright
the waters blinked a million shimmering lights:
stretched far as eyes could see
into the deep open sea.

I remembered the days of old
in a village nestled on the bank of the sea.
A child with outstretched palms
stood before that mighty unruffled calm.
Marveled whence those sparkles came.
But then—
in my little heart contained,
like on a tiny screen—
awesome stretches of stars seen.

My Childhood Days

I remember my childhood days.
The pond on the playing field
where I held a string of tadpoles,
like a garland of black pearls.
Where I sent my little Nina, Pinta, and Santa Maria
to seas wide and far,
and they brought spices and gems
from splendid isles I long dreamt.

I remember my childhood days.
Yellow-breasted kiskadees flitted
and sang on branches all day.
Sweet melodies drifted far away.
Their beaks pierced sun-ripened mangoes
that glowed with a yellow hue.
Cherries, gooseberries, guavas, and star apples
I gathered near hammock under the shed.
Then lulled by mild wind to blissful rest.

I remember my childhood days.
The crackling canes on fire,
flying ash, flames leaping higher:
an explosive volcano in miniature.
And when the fiery show was over,
we ran to the fields to gather
joints made sweeter by the fire.

Tied in bundles on slender shoulders.
We ripped their skins—
every drop of juice from flesh drained.

I remembered my childhood days.
The fresh red bruises on knees,
layers of hardened mud on feet—
inscriptions of the hills I wheeled, woods I roamed,
when sun and rains scarcely found me alone.

Watched tides battered the shore.
When by degrees their fury subsided,
the wearied men of the sea
lowered their nets in depths I had longed to be.

I remembered the misty perfume of the wind.
The curious shells, rounded rocks,
memories gathered along the shore
where the soft ethereal music of the sea
whispered to my soul and made me free.

The Deep Open Sea

She watches little crafts with colorful sails.
Men in trawlers harpoon blue whales—
miles of blood from deliberate cruel will, unlike a spill,
ruffles her face with the trail of those who kill.

Makes giddy, armadas, liners, and merchant ships,
a little anger she could flounder and set adrift.
She is the open sea that swells in pristine majesty,
and untold stories of primordial bones and shells.

Many an ancient city on her bosom rest.
What treasures and secrets she has kept.
Ill-fated ships and sailors haunt her depths.
Great rings of fire adorn her breasts.

Mariners of yore heeded her call.
Sails unfurled for lands near and afar.
And along the shore her lingering voice—
when the surf breathes into the silence of the night.

Some Unfinished Work

I once knew these fields I roam,
these hills I kiss,
these lush pastures,
these restless streams.

I once knew the old churchyard
overgrown with vines and weeds.
The dam the sea has breached,
these coconut palms swaying in the breeze.

Even these faces seem familiar,
the muddy roads, bushes, and flowers.
The very wind whispers to my soul:
"You have been here before."

But like an errant schoolboy
some unfinished work to complete.
Some lesson to learn
before my spirit again moves on.

And where I go from here:
never written or told,
not privy to the earth or the stars.
I travel beyond their purview—afar

What Manner of Hand

What manner of hand
that taps the shoulders of a tiny seed
to rise and grow into a giant oak tree.
That lifts a drowsy shoot
to stand in the light of the sun,
and spreads a carpet of green
to know it's the vernal season around.

What manner of hand
that carved mountains, dug seas and oceans.
That scattered sands in the vast deserts,
made rivers furrowed deep into the land—
great canyons to born.

What manner of hand
that paints the red on a robin's breast,
and iridescent colors on wings of a butterfly.
Fills heavenly fragrance in a gardenia,
guides the beaver to build a dam,
and beckons the wind to calm.

What manner of hand
that laid orbits of planets and stars.
That fashioned that vaulted blue,
writes blinding forks of light,
and armed the cobra with venom to strike.

What manner of hand
that sends cascades from rocks high,
a banded ribbon arching the sky.
Plants into the womb an embryo strong—
a child for the world to smile.
Weaves a web of silence
that envelopes the breath of eternity,
and places in the human heart:
the light of a million stars.

Invisible

An invisible wound
crawls deep with a sunken feeling that flays—
unrelenting knocks on the citadels of the mind.
A resolute will pleads for it to heal.
It acquiesces but only after it has drained
every glass of wine of the richness of its flavor.

Invisible deep throbbing pain at fault lines bursting
when earth opens her mouth and swallows buildings.
An invisible ghastly impulse in a tyrant's heart.
Flowers of a fair world besmirched.
The marching drums of hate and strife,
and rivers rushing with blood

An invisible thought illuminates a path.
What terror holds the dark?
It's a blinding torch.
The world's on the march,
when an invisible thought breaks servile bonds,
and like the sun floods hearts with songs.

Invisible exultation in the heart of the poet
to paint in words:
springs gushing from the earth,
Autumn's leaves like flowers under our feet,
a string of pearls from the ocean gathered,

fallen feathers from falcon's flight.

Don't Give Up on the World

Don't give up on the world.
Don't say it has never been worse.
We have come a long way
from those rivers of blood,
blighted seasons from the beetles' infernal deeds,
discordant drums, flags that blazoned vile creeds,

When wretched echoes invade your dreams,
and spoil sweet hours of the day,
they are along the bending ways,
from caverns dark and deep.
Take comfort we will see the sun again—
resplendent along the world's beaten paths.

Unseen They Roam

The smell of newly dug earth
mingles with the air unspoiled.
The smell of freshly cut green grass,
hot tar laid on a stretch of road,
or to make sturdy timbers of a boat.
The pungent odor of peeled onions.
The sweet blast of leaves of mint and basil—
floods deck and porch with stories to tell.

The aroma of corn bread in the oven,
a cheesy zucchini casserole,
pumpkin pies and tarts of pineapple,
popcorn and roasted nuts laced with honey.
And drifting out of the windows,
inviting trail of fried plantains and sweet potatoes.

The fragrance of the blooming jasmines,
colorful hyacinths, rich chrysanthemums,
tender gardenias, proud pink Asiatic lilies,
lotuses rising undefiled in the muddy wild.
The scent of a summer's breeze
mixed with leaves, mud, and twigs.

Unseen they roam,
but not with the freedom of the wind
that gives them wings.

Yet—
they fashion my dreams, awaken my desires.
Leave their imprint on my shoulders
after I passed the limits of their purview,
like the freshness of the spray
that lingers in my breast
long after I crossed the margin of the bay—
to contemplate the passing of the day.

Unknown

A song gushes from the heart of an unknown singer
in a railway station in an obscure corner.
No rhythms of drums, no clash of cymbals,
no discordant beat on a broken table.
Nothing but her voice to lift sweet song
that rises above the wails of hurried trains,
far, far beyond the distant enchanted plains.

Unknown wildflowers sit on beleaguered fences.
Unspoiled paths sheltered from the city's noises.
No one plucks them for a splendid vase.
They adorn the hair of no maiden fair.
They smile on no lovely bouquet.
But their fragrance rises over hills and rivers,
like the trail of a flock of falcons floating free.

Unknown names engraved on no granite wall.
No camera lights intrude their nights and days.
Their likeness splash on no tabloid page.
But their hands heal wounds deep and grave.
Lift with a loaf of bread, a cup of hot cereal,
and wipe many a river of tears.

The unknown star an enigma afar.
The unknown frontier an irresistible call.
Yet the unknown we fear.

But every leap made,
the unknown put to the blade.
And when we dive in unknown deep waters,
rare gems and pearls are gathered.

The unknown heart who walks alone
with the quiet of untrodden paths.
Sits on bare grass,
gazes at the sun fading fast,
and recites with fervor,
like blood rushing in the veins—
unsung verses of a poet.

Life is Better on the Porch

Life is better on the porch.
No dark curtains to hide
familiar faces, hands raised—
greetings to infuse the day with hours sweet.
The wind brings fragrance of the hyacinth.
The sun blasts the fever away.
Clouds over your head hang.
Eyes roam on the wings of a gliding falcon.

Life is better on the porch.
The mailman comes with a smile.
Talks of grave and funny things for a while.
You feel like a child at heart
when laughter of children rises from the park.
You watch squirrels mount the trees with glee.
Wish you were as nimble and free,
but glad on the porch—watch gulls circle the clouds.

A Host of Stars Bright

The world fast asleep.
I gazed at the still night's sky.
Saw in the Milky Way a host of stars bright
looking down with longing eyes.
A deep feeling more than an awareness,
like when one looks at a child's face,
as I gazed and gazed with wonder great.

My heart reached those blithe spirits.
Homage from awesome stretches of space.
How tiny this splendid orb we dwell,
their vision beyond the cosmic veil,
and what realms they contain, what lies beyond—
eyes probe the deep as stars are born.

Like flakes of snow, such frailty we show.
But some rare unearthly flower blooms
with fragrance deep in our hearts and souls—
a galactic odyssey for that host of stars
whirling through limitless space and skies:
smiling with adoring eyes.

A Different Feeling, A Different World

While we walk along pristine beaches,
gilded streets in splendid cities,
there's a different feeling, a different world:
those who trek miles along muddy paths
for a bucket of water before day turns dark.

While our tables are filled with food and wine
gathered from the best of fields and vineyards,
there's a different feeling, a different world:
those with bodies emaciated for want of bread
when living becomes worse than death.

While we snuggle within layers of comfort and smiles,
dream of pretty maidens and distant isles,
there's a different feeling, a different world:
children who in piteous cries admonish the stars.
Limbs that kiss cold concrete on which tears have dried.

While we dwell in the garden of fame and beauty,
watch sun-drenched clouds and the placid blue sea,
there's a different feeling, a different world:
those who crawl out of a rubble to wake
up in a city of tents with disfigured faces of orphans.

Patterns

Behold the veins
etched on
a maple leaf.

Those stretched
to a network
in the body.

The green tendrils
of a grape vine,
shell of a mollusk.

Horns of the antelope,
florets of the sunflower,
bands of a dreaded cyclone.

DNA strands
in a twisted ladder,
arms of the Milky Way.

The patterns
in nature replicate.
Geometry of beauty abounds.

And if made into music:
a symphony of ineffable

   power and harmony

would rush,
and flood
the human heart.

Spinning Wheels

The world reckons they just keep going.
They're spinning wheels.
When they kiss for hours miles of sprawling
asphalt and tar,
and long, narrow, resolute steel bars.
Not when sitting at ease,
their nature knows no such peace.

When all the world's a race,
why wheels of unruffled, cold faces?
They were born to impress the roads.
A screech, a trail of wet ribbon,
a quick dash, a turn, miles to burn.
To sink their teeth into soft ground,
hug the rails with hurried beats of drums.

They carry scars of sharp rocks.
When there is impending danger
they raise the dust higher,
and burn with a blistering fever.
They too suffer abuse and neglect.
Even spinning wheels—
need some rest.

Blighted Flowers

Beleaguered light in the pupil of their eyes:
barred windows, sagging fences,
concrete walls of fear and hate.
In a landscape of nightmares
they live and die.
No romance, trees of palm,
picnic by the lake, walking to the farm.
But!
rapid bursts of gunfire,
blood splashed on walls,
sirens, screams, friends slain,
or behind portentous bars.

On street corners and dark corridors
peddlers of greed and death open their wares.
Temptations rattle in sinister stares.
The young cry for help,
but it's a world callous and deaf.
When in every cup the taste of gall,
even a will of steel will stumble and fall,
and like fields of corn in the beetles' infernal path,
the flowers of youth will droop in morbid blight.

The Mango Tree

In sunshine and rains, it stood elegant and tall.
Branches brushed against windows and wall.
A canopy over a hammock to rest and sleep.
Roots like tentacles stretched to buckle concrete—
the mango tree that lingers deep in my breast.

Its leaves sprinkled the sacred waters.
Hang on brocaded tents of weddings.
Strung artistically around the mouth
of the ritually decorated earthen pot,
and boiled in water over gentle fire—
a potent drink for the rigors of fever.

The mango tree in the yard.
The kiskadee flitted from branch to branch.
Sweet melodies mingled with tender breeze.
We mounted its trunk; rested on branches strong—
when days were pregnant with boyhood pranks.

The branches of the mango tree bowed
with oval-shaped fruits ripened by the sun.
With bamboo sticks we prodded at the stems
of those that smiled from branches high.
Some were caught before they kissed the ground.
The glee greater than any treasure found.

Some hid their faces in narrow drains.
No less savored though mud stained.
When the kiskadee pierced their red-yellow armor,
they glowed; they grew sweeter by the hour.
But sweetest of all—
those that fell of their own accord,
and laid like ambrosia to the eyes.

Breath of an Uneasy Wind

The waters of the lake
so calm, so clear—
can see a white pebble
deep down there.

The trees beside the margin of the lake
painted on a broad watery canvas—
every branch, twig, and leaf finely drawn
by a master artist of tireless hand.

But the unwelcome breath of an uneasy wind,
a sudden agitation brings.
A strife that mars the bliss:
a wretched embrace, a dreadful kiss.

Wonder how the wind can be so mean
to trouble a lake serene—
not even a boulder asleep within
seen by eyes strong and keen.

The Masks

The masks we wear:
smiles that hold a sea of tears,
or laced with the venom of a cobra.
Fashioned with subtlety and guile
from the limbs and sinews of the self
that cannot stand naked in the wind—
in just being,
but ever seeks
creeping shadows in the woods deep,
and will travel ten thousand leagues
from the face of the sun
to the comfort of dark caverns.

The masks we wear,
changing colors of the chameleon,
hide us from the world.
To tear them one by one,
costumes stretched to sea and land.
It's how far we have gone
to put this masquerade on.
But then—
we would bask in the glory of the sun.
Hear the sweet rhythms of the sea.
Watch the leaves of Autumn,
like butterflies alighted on branches.
Embrace the clouds that roll pass,

and kiss the earth that wears no mask.

Miracles

When the blind can see again.
Follow a gazelle on the far-flung plains.
When the lame can scale resplendent cliffs.
Smile and sing as the wind lifts.
When malignant tentacles dug in blood and marrow
vanished like insects snatched by a swallow—
we proclaim these as miracles indeed,
and in exultation begin to believe.

But miracles everywhere abound.
In a gentle stroll if we stop to look around.
As when a gull cuts the air with wings outstretched.
A beautiful rainbow arches over the sky.
A constellation of stars hangs on a branch.
The hummingbird kisses deep a honeysuckle flower.
The shore stretches a distant mile,
and when it's all covered as we dance and smile.

Gorges

It was wrought over the ages.
A river carved into layers of primordial rocks,
and when time did bid its savage artistry to stop—
on Earth's fair face a deep wide gash.
But!
What a majestic ornament made:
the Grand Canyon in breathtaking wonder we gaze.

In our lives are gorges gaping —
cut into the ramparts of our being
with ruthless blows of mighty cunning streams.
We rue the cruel plot time had weaved.
If only that river had not carved so deep.
But like that rough gash on Earth's fair face—
time may have wrought us ornaments of grace.

Memories of the Ocean

Along a shore in a far country
my heart floods with distant memories.
Refreshing breeze of the irrepressible Atlantic
that wafted over my little village.
The castles I built that waves dismantled.
Woods and branches that drifted in aimless bundles.

When the sun rose with a golden smile,
I gazed at the dance of water and light.
An unearthly calm in the ocean's tranquil mood.
Waves caressed the sand as in a musical interlude,
and when in convulsion they battered the shore—
mighty surges thundered and drenched my soul.

I watched the beaten wall ceded in places.
Rocks and timbers worn by water and slime.
Roofs of zinc corroded with the salty mist.
Fences that sagged to kiss the grass.
Stared at houses with tales of climbing vines,
and limbs and sinews in haunted decline,
but that watery realm below the vaulted blue—
untouched by time.

If there's a thing that lingers in my breast,
it's the call of the ocean that knows no rest.
Its mystical notes echo in my dreams—

rapture of a silence that invades my being.
And when I sit in a meditative mood:
the ocean rides with waves that soothe.

Every Throbbing Heart

What's the labor in every walk, ramble, and climb
if the pure fragrance of earth enters not the mind?
If we feel not the breath in every blade of grass,
every crab we search, every throbbing heart.

Why strain for that effulgent orb climbing the horizon
if the inward eye probes not its eternal radiance?
Robins and sparrows sing in treetops day long.
Have strings within awakened a finer song?

There's more in a journey to far-flung places,
thrill of riding waves, sailing high in a canopy.
It's the magical calm and melody of the deep blue sea,
bending palm trees that linger long in memory.

It Watches in Silence

There's something within
that watches in silence.
At night and during the day
when the clouds turn gray,
and when the sky's all blue.
When a desert waste I see,
and a sea of yellow tulips dance before me.

Like a celestial bird of golden plumage
perched on a treetop high,
it watches the seasons roll,
and the tides rise and fall.
It sees the cobra lifting its head,
and a dog fetching a loaf of bread.

It looks at babbling brooks,
and loathsome dried-up ponds.
Dolphins riding waves,
a stranded whale on shore in tears.
Frolicsome breeze of spring,
and blast of winter's arctic winds.

It sees the marching drums of anger.
Children raising their voices in a choir.
It looks at refugees in tents of agony,
and in halls of power where spoils are garnered.

It sees the wastelands of vile deeds,
and fields of green farmers labor and reap.

Often wonder what it is
that so blissfully rests within.
But deep in my breast
I pray I may take some hint
from this supernal thing,
and perhaps be like it too—
that watches in silence serene.

My Garden of Flowers

My little garden resplendent with diverse flowers.
Roses, tulips, azaleas, lilies, and petunias,
black, white, red, yellow, pink, and blue,
smiling under the shade of a far-flung tree.

I watch how they kiss, hug, and rally.
Blend beyond the margins of the fragrance they carry.
How they sway and dance in the breeze,
and lift their faces every passerby to greet.

Spirits down by scorching sun, rains, and cruel winds.
Bruised and forlorn, but like spires they rise—
animated by a bond like reeds in a raging storm,
and smile and dance to the newborn morn.

I imagine the world as my little garden of flowers.
No domestic walls of hate to despoil the landscape.
Hands of diverse colors uplifted to care and share.
A blending of all as we smile, sing, dance, and toil.

I imagine the world as my little garden of flowers.
Freedom sings on treetops all day long.
And when the radiance of the sun floods sea and land—
it's a world shaped by every color of hands.

A Wretched Wind

A wretched wind brought a baffling insidious thing
in every land and clime to spread its virulent wings.
And ere long a wasteland of lonely, tortured screams.
The shroud of silence falls like frost on petunias.
Will that care-free laughter be the same?
Will the world sing and dance again?

Now I fear my fellow beings,
as if in every breath this macabre thing.
In the streets I hide my face.
It may lurk in any place.
I scarce venture in the city's thoroughfares—
its wings may lightly brush me unaware.

I am scared to touch the knob of a door.
There the invader may rest secure.
Even an innocent flower holds a menace
if a human finger has embraced it.
And to the vigilance of daily living,
the ritual of exorcising this dreaded thing.

I sit quietly and read of adventures at sea,
tropical isles, coral reefs, and bending palm trees—
a diversion to quiet the pulse of obsessive care.
It takes me to the crowded open air,
the festive beat of drums—

the life I knew before that wretched wind blew
.

The Threads Interwoven

The days that swiftly rolled away,
like mist lifted and gone.
Like flowers faded and fallen
whose fragrance the winds have carried
beyond the plains over the sea.

The days to come
like hopes of a maiden.
Buds where smiles are hidden.
Like infant wrapped in a cozy womb.
Warm beach on a summer's day
while winter bites with stinging winds,
or oak tree sealed in the earth,
someday to straddle the clouds.

But today—
blooming petals of spring,
light of the resplendent sun
invading hill, field, and stream around.
In its brief span—
the threads interwoven
into the fabric
of every breath and pulse,
every taste, color, and sound,
every rushing water and wind,
every flapping wing—

every splendor and beauty:
the universe and its intriguing mystery.

Look at Nature

Nature cares not—
screams of unrelenting pain or shouts of joy,
the depravity or the virtue,
the wretchedness or the beaming smiles,

The fragrance of the hyacinth
reaches the heart of the adulteress,
and the chaste wife.
The river washes killer's hands smeared with blood.
Carries an earthen lamp of clay offered by a pilgrim.
Sun's rays fall on the crown of the tyrant.
Flowing robe of the sage.
Mild wind drifts into the huts of poor.
Ornate windows of the affluent.
Stars watch over the homeless on pavements.
Merchants who sip vintage wines in mansions.

Nature knows not the ways of humans
who exclude, who stratify,
delight in layers of caste and purity.
Make images of the Divine into untouchables
whose shadows pollute the pure in lineage,
and whose hands were made to keep the fires ablaze
on ceremonially clad bodies along the riverbanks.

No separate wells on nature's breast.
No high wall spikes, razor wire fences.
No flags that segregate and despise,
and blazon the claims of clan and tribe.
Behold how the redwoods embrace and kiss.
The shared patterns of bliss their roots interweave.

When the marching drums of disdain resound
look! look at nature!
Pours her heart in profuse strains of joy—
the bounty of her fields in grains and herbs,
and kisses the very hands that defile her:
a mother who embraces all.

Oak Trees and Reeds

Oak trees reach for the clouds.
They yield not, nor bow
to stormy winds that rage and howl.
Roots that crawl deep in earth
make them strong, but proud.
To think they can face the tempest's blast,
the winds' anger and fury to outlast.
But who would wager on their fate against
a power that rocks the sea to frenzied waves.
The oaks shaken, battered, and bruised,
like wounded soldiers on a ghastly field.
Some uprooted on a broad mortuary slab
when winds teared the land with a grisly dance.

But slender reeds along the river's edge
bow and yield at the winds' behest.
When the winds in vexation roar,
the reeds yield and bend even more.
Dance with the suppleness of a ballerina
as the storm rages over.
Quick to kiss the ground,
the world to reckon they are done.
But their humility the crown to deeds renown.

And when it's all over,

and waters run from lush pastures,
the gentle reeds upright as ever—
sway to another morn, another song of the robin.

Dark Depths of the Sea

With heavy nets I probed the sea's depths,
but save for slippery fishes, pebbles, and weeds,
never revealed the secret of her pristine majesty.

What mysteries lie beneath the waves
deep, deep, deep.
Like a candle in the dark that flickers and dies,
light fades and fades into a universe pitch dark.
A perpetual night that knows no respite
envelopes the sea with the breath of eternity.

But when the sunken night looks up,
beholds stars bright, constellations, a Milky Way,
shimmering lights from bizarre jellyfishes and squids,
and creatures whimsical in the wild dark deep.

There are eyes probing beyond the vaulted blue,
crowds of galaxies in deep, deep, deep space.
We hear music and sounds countless eons made.
But the sights and melodies in the deeper sea,
an agonizing, bewildering mystery.
No less in awe than the mariners of yore—
will the secrets below ever be told?

Heart of a Child

We see the sun rising.
Another day wears the mind,
a foreboding of what's to come.
But it floods the heart of a child
who sees only its smiles,
not the hours it rides,
and when it quietly slips away—
plays on walls with shadows big and tall.

Slightest tap on roof,
we close windows, bring curtains down.
A child opens its heart
to every drop of rain that falls,
every stream, every pond that awakens a song.
And when the showers are over
launches ships to far off corners,
builds dams and sends tides away.

Our steps wearied,
heavy burdens we carry.
Our fears and worries
like boulders on a delicate canopy.
But like confetti in the wind,
light is the heart of a child,
sparkles with songs and wonder,
rush of innocent laughter.

The broad canvas stretched wide,
but we no longer see
delicate strokes and flourishes
wild in the heart of a child:
spider's web sparkling in the sunshine,
a constellation of stars strung on a branch.
A wren's nest on the fork of a tree—
too delicate a basket human hands to weave.

We huddle close to our kind
like merchandise on a shelf.
The circle the heart reaches
circumscribed by the familiar tribe.
In the heart of a child
the rhythms and songs
of strange drums and voices,
adventures and tales from far-off places.

We delight in rites, rituals, and ceremonies,
layers of caste and racial purity.
We cling like barnacles to sunken timbers—
blazoned flags and banners of hate and strife
in strident marches to proclaim our slumber.
But a child brims with smiles sweet,
and sees not the color of the lips
kissing waters gushing from a spring.

Oh! how close the heart of a child
to a clear stream in the wild.
If we can enter a child's heart,

the rolling hills, the distant plains
would never be the same.
In the child's heart is a poet, a guide,
a teacher, a seer to open the inward eye.

We reason, we analyze too much.
The strings of the heart we little pluck.
Is it not enough to delight
in the fragrance of the flower?
But we crush its petals,
extract the oil and scent,
and bottled it to a world
lost to the call of the wild.
But to the heart of a child,
every petal is a temple of love.

Butterfly on My Shoulder

When I was young
fleet-footed and strong
I ran after a butterfly
that flitted with wings of scarlet sunset,
and iridescent marks of blue and green.

When I fancied it within my grasp
it gathered speed and lifted fast,
and not once on my fingers impressed
the golden dust of a delicate fabric,
steadied by the music of celestial strings.

But now at last, I sit and wait,
a heart less in beat and haste
gazing at the clouds and the lake.
And as if drawn by an invisible thread at sunrise—
the butterfly on my shoulder alights.

A Felt Exultation

The sea that washes the wide shore,
sweet to hear it once more.
Who can be tired of its charms?
Every hour it's the eternal rush or calm.
When it's in deep rest,
not a wrinkle in its face so fresh—
there's a sound no human or bird,
or thing that dwells or glances over earth
can match in fullness and mirth.

A sound so soft, yet so deep,
can take one as if to sleep.
But not the sleep
that overpowers tired body and mind,
but one with wings
that transport to realms sublime—
where profuse strains
of yet softer, deeper strings
awaken a felt exultation in one's being.

The Love of a Mother

It was a dismal day.
With no hearth and home
he hobbled in a tattered coat along the dingy road.
The dogs barked at him with menacing eyes.
The rains lashed at his disheveled face.
In the wind's tempestuous roar,
echoes of a tortured diary
where the only friends he knew—
the pangs of hunger, a heart distempered.

He looked long and hard.
Nowhere could he find
a place to rest body and mind.
He came to the end of the road.
He looked beyond,
and longed for the warmth
of the old farmhouse he was born.

He summoned the remnants of a decayed resolve.
Lumbered along a winding faded path
of neglected fields and sagging fences.
The old farmhouse glistened in the failing day.
He knocked long until he fell on the steps,
and as if from heaven's open door
he heard the words, "Oh my son!"

The hands that held him once rocked his cradle.
Sung many a lullaby that made him smiled.
Gently tucked the sheet under his tender body.
Beckoned the stars to watch over his sleep.
They soothed his blisters and wounds
with the incomparable balm of a mother's love,
and when the nights were dark
held him close to heart.

She fed him the corn bread he favored.
It appeased more than his hunger:
it was heavenly ambrosia.
Those hands held him again close to heart.
Unto his mind came the thought
mixed with tears, and overflowing joy—
the love of a mother
like the pure waters of a gushing spring
can soothe a heart most wretched and worn.

A Higher Call

Who can tell a robin where to build a nest,
what grass, twigs, leaves to put to test?
Behold one of nature's great architects.
A cozy pouch on fork of a tree,
built to withstand the wind's wrath and fury.
Wherein the young embolden with fragile wings,
long in the woods to roam and sing.
Ride with the winds over the sea,
mount the sky majestic and free.

Who can counsel a nightingale to stretch a note?
It sings to a higher call in courtyards and fields remote.
Tides too know when to rise and fall.
The chrysalis when to release a delicate winged fabric.
A rattlesnake knows when to shed its skin.
A peacock when to open its iridescent fan.
The vines on which derelict fence to climb,
and the river where to linger with a smile—
where to rush like an untamed horse in the wild.

One Day at a Time

One day at a time:
life of a grain of sand,
earthworm that wriggles like an accordion,
rabbit in a cozy den underground,
giant star that burns its life out.

One day at a time:
life of the tiny seed
through the span of winter sleeps.
Snails that cling to rocks with a tenacious embrace.
Gourds that bristled with bitter warts,
ocean that shouts for songs of humpback whale.

One day at a time:
life of the creeping vines
that would not leave the beleaguered fence.
Wild geraniums with pretty blooms under the pines.
Swans with necks entwined in a love heart,
walrus that sports moustache smart.

One day at a time:
drums of woodpeckers, strings of manakins proclaim,
signpost in garden, mountain peak, valley, and stream,
and the bruised face of the red hibiscus heals
no faster—thinking of rain-borne clouds tomorrow.

A Cable of Steel

At the first whisper of morn
he weaved and weaved strand by strand.
The voice within admonished in vain.
He took a liking to what he had weaved.
It took root; it held strong,
and ere long a dreaded habit born.

Like a strange vile thing unseen,
an ominous shadow haunted his being.
Gone that smile, that robust frame.
He lumbered with a disheveled face.
And those who once knew him,
wondered what ill made him so lean.

A feverish thirst took over his mind.
Futile to make him understand—
he gathered more strands.
He wrapped them around each other,
and with such a tight embrace
not even the wind could see their faces.

He daily fed this habit long.
He groaned and stumbled at its command.
No protest within his breast arose.
The clear stream within all but choked.
That dreaded thing delighted in his decline—

plundered the citadels of his mind.

One day he looked out of his window.
He saw a lone sparrow on a treetop.
It sang; he listened long.
A rare ray of light entered his mind.
He summoned a beleaguered will,
but his habit was a cable of steel.

Restless Longing

In my restless longing
I tried to comprehend life
in gilded pages on dusty shelves,
discourses and invocations,
and aphorisms like distilled wine.

But little light in my heart shines
along a road despairing and lonely—
whilst the earth wakes
with a thousand rhythms of joy,
sun blazes on lush paddy fields,
and life rolls with an irresistible charm

beckoning to look no further beyond:
tender green shoots greeting dawn,
trees bending, looking over pond.
The rapture of a nightingale's song.
Lark soaring into clouds of crimson golden hues.
Rivers rushing to embrace the sea.
The firmament on a still dark night—
mighty sprawling trees adorned with lights.

Numbers

They have a magic and an allure.
Show on their faces for sure.
With no life of their own
behold how they reveal and track
the signs of life in their ebb and flow.
The age of the universe and a microbe,
the orbital paths of planets and stars—
when we will see Halley's comet in the night's sky.

We take their cue when to sleep and wake,
another dose of medicine to take.
When the needle point to their steady rise,
a fever may disclose a malady inside.
They tell of which day to celebrate,
which from memory to obliterate.
They hold secrets of layers of stones,
and of primordial shells and bones.

When they wake up like blinding dust
on paper, screen, or board—
we may not see how they fall or rise.
But if we make them into pictures,
jets lifting off, gulls plunging into the waters,
waves rippling or tormenting the shore,
little drums, or chimneys that loudly snore—
they tell us so much more.

They disclose in their smiles or chagrin
the labor's loss or gain.
When they stand united and strong,
it's the time to redress a wrong.
Mighty blows to powers and principalities
when the city's gates they throng.
When alone they reveal a little wonder:
there's much strength in numbers.

My Ancestors

Fields of green stretched far as eyes could see.
They swayed and danced in the lively breeze.
But a river of tears they held,
and the blood and sweat of my ancestors
who toiled from dawn to the vanished charms
of twilight—a thing bitter sweet to born.

They endured the ocean's wrath, the winds' blast.
A journey to a distant land—
their dreams dashed on the sands.
But like the canes they held in bundles tight,
forged a bond in the day and night
with the drums and songs of their native land.

In the shadow of the taskmaster's wretched gaze
they labored; they heard the crack of whips.
Their blood like canes ablazed,
appeased with silent tears.
Roped strands of pain engraved on a brother's back,
and impressed in hearts that bled.

They trembled in flooded long barrack-like huts
from virulent knocks of wretched visitors:
dreaded cholera, dysentery, and dengue fever.
And when they ventured from cramped quarters,
gazed in awe at white mansions of the taskmasters:

another world apart—bitter sweet sugar had wrought.

A Virus

When gentle nature
reveals a ghastly feature—
brings pains and screams
from most minute of things.

Often replicates
in ways too subtle to know,
to baffle the best
of human knowledge and probe.

As when a virus veers
from the familiar track
to hide for a while along
a dark and forbidden path.

Then to emerge at the ramparts
of the enemies' stronghold—
with grisly weapons
for a prolonged deadly attack.

A Serpentine Foe

In the silence of a starless night
a serpentine foe slithered
into the city of Wuhan.
The dance of death began.
A nervous world held its breath—
the enigma of an enemy
no weapon, no missile can impede.

Never such fear and unease
since the Spanish flu, the dreaded polio,
the first shot heard in Sarajevo,
the fascists' march into the Rhineland,
the occupation of Montenegro.

Teheran, Rome, and Milan locked
in the vise-like grip of its jaws.
A somber mood the call to prayers
in the cities of Medina and Mecca.
No gathering of pilgrims at the holy Kaaba.

It struck hard at the heart
of boisterous London, Paris, and New York.
The bull repeatedly stumbled on its face—
sent global shock waves.
The world like a ravaged shore—
the enemy struck rich and poor.

Then waves of a social tsunami,
upheavals in towns and communities.
Goals scored, and balls hurled into baskets,
but no spectator stood up and applauded.
Lessons were taught in the clouds.
The refrain—
wear mask, wash hands, and avoid the crowds.

A Dream

Spring walked into my dream:
melodies of the red-breasted robin and the canary,
the freshness of running streams, aroma
of earth mixed with grass, twigs, and leaves,
exotic perfume of the gardenia,
red and yellow tulips, daffodils like golden trumpets.
A seed that slept through the winter
burst into blooming large white lilies,
and everywhere I turned
the festival of colors around.

I looked at the faces of people.
Blank pages impressed with fear.
No exultation and cheers
as Spring laid out her bountiful fare.
Where music once blared at thoroughfares,
an eerie silence fills the air,
as the shadow of death marches
into every land and clime.

No hurried feet trampled the pavements.
No crowd gazed at the giant screens.
No frenzied rush to work or play.
No parades, no festive beat of drums.
No applause, no encore.
A somber mood took hold.

The bustle of teeming cities
vanished like the mist at dawn.
The boisterous rivers ceased to flow.

I saw people in dark caverns,
and many who carried the light
the world to pass this dreaded night.
I saw hands that knew no rest.
Never felt a bond so strong—
the human family we belong.

I roused from the dream.
It was no longer a dream,
but the world straddled in pain before my eyes.

How Long?

How long a warm handshake,
and a cough and a sneeze be so feared?
How long a crowd to hold such harm,
and cries of battle and sirens go on?

How long a city that never sleeps,
the likeness of a locomotive stalled?
How long these days and nights of pains and cries,
the agony of a lonely death; funerals with no rites?

How long no parades, no revelry, no beat
of festive drums, stadiums with empty seats?
How long the foreboding to cross the seas,
and ride in a gondola on the canals of Venice?

How long these grim charts,
from a plateau jets taking off?
How long the fear to hug a dear aunt,
the caution to embrace a cherished friend?

How long this dread of our own kind,
this obsessive care, this nightmare?
How long the weary world in wait
to sing and dance, and sleep in ease again?

Every wait seems too long,

but the scourge baffling and strong.
Hope rides on every fear, every wait.
Rests not on shifting sands of fate,
but on the bedrock of human ingenuity,
firm as a giant sequoia tree.
And the arrow of the probing mind
released by the hands of time—
a mighty blow to the enemy's fortress,
a mighty relief for the world in wait.

I Feel the Pain

When you lie with cough and fever high,
struggle for air that fills earth and sky.
Tubes in nostrils, mouth, and veins,
stricken by an invisible enemy unyielding—
know that I feel your every pain.
I kneel and bow for you to walk again,
smile in the sun, and dance in the rain.

The children who cry for want of food,
mothers, fathers who bind wounds fresh and deep—
I wish this were only a dream.
A nightmare that overslept.
A sad refrain for the mood to lift,
like the moon in blood in a rare eclipse,
that emerges with a brighter smile.

Three Rivers

A river flows
with swift, sly currents and cunning billows.
Washes the shore
with broken limbs of trees, splintered woods,
scattered debris of dark memories,
treasured colorful shells of forgotten joys.

Another river plays on the shore
with waves that ripple with dreams never told,
and desires that never cease to flow.
But more often lashes with furious,
frightful waves churned by portentous winds
that rattle the calm within.

But there is a third river
we scarce visit or enter.
Brings to the shore gems precious and rare.
Inexpressible joy of just watching it flowing,
and listening to its silent whisperings—
echoes of musical strings within.

Music

Music to the human heart—
a greater feeling for ineffable things:
gushing springs in a lover's heart,
freedom of a falcon gliding over a restless sea,
serenity of the stars watching over our sleep,
majestic beauty of snow-capped mountain peaks

Beyond voices and lyrics, rhythms of drums and strings,
music surging like fresh air of spring.
Taking the mind to babbling brooks, rushing streams,
a magical garden in an enchanted dream.
In the heart's inn no room for a dreary day,
the sun's out when sweet music we play.

Music like a most welcome passing wind
breathing over and gentle shaking
dispirited drowsy dust and jaded trees.
And forlorn human hearts sweetly chiming,
wearied minds rising over hills, fields of wine
to drums racing, cymbals clashing, strings trembling.

Music mounting over our wonted dwellings,
beyond the clouds, reaching the gates of heaven.
Like a visitor from an unearthly realm,
revealing what's more worthy than precious gems—
the breath of the Eternal: ceaseless cosmic rhythms.

How We Treat Our Feathered Friends

Neat packages on shivering shelves,
but they hide from our eyes
chickens cramped in tiny wire cages,
standing in their feces near decaying bodies.
Never seen the light that dances on the lake.
Never kissed the earth with their beaks.
Their feathers never ruffled by a cool breeze.
Never took a dust bath,
as nature impressed in their hearts.
Never walked on soft green grass,
golden leaves downed by Autumn's blast.

Stabbed by syringes to fatten for our banquets.
Stunned by machines that slit
their throats in a fast-moving line.
Those that missed the blade and left behind,
boiled to death in feather removal tanks.
But are these not our feathered friends?
Are these not sentient beings
that like to crow and cluck and brood and grumble,
flock together in a pecking order?
Their blood too is of the same color—
their hearts beat with the same primordial desires.

Condos & High-Rises

There's a change in the face, a new look
to the placid town I once knew.
Derelict buildings razed to the ground,
condos, towers in the clouds abound.
The blue draped horizon painfully shrouded
by sprawling giants frozen in the sky.
Ribs of steel tightly drawn in style.
Glass, concrete, and granite stretched upward a mile.
The noise of machines, the endless traffic—
trees stand forlorn and blighted.

Another street, another side walk cordoned off.
The caterpillar machines disfigured the ground.
These strange people around—
developers with a turn for quick profit in town.
Seems the cranes would never go home.
All over this once quiet town they roam.
Drone of concrete mixers, rude staccato
of jackhammers invade the sanctity
of church bells that chime the hours.
And that golden orb blazing the sky
hidden by a distorted face from a distant high.

The feet that pound the pavements
speak of a restlessness, a haste,
a new zeal—the world their mark to make.

The quiet sounds of languid strings
yield to throbbing beat of boisterous drums.
The congenial atmosphere of the corner store
make way for upscale cafes and yoga studios.
The smell of a new affluence around,
like a surging sea devouring this cherished town—
gone for good in all but in its name.

Lift Your Mind

Lift your mind to the deep blue sky,
scattered clouds sedately passing by.
Mountains resting in obdurate ease.
Canopy of bamboo leaves in rain forest deep.
Gulls that blaze a trail of glory over the sea.

Lift your mind to waters tumbling from rocks.
Bridge that arches with colors from a prism scattered.
Stars at night beckoning with smiles.
Aurora Borealis, magic on northern skies,
the enchanting flight of the tiger moth butterfly,

Lift your mind to fields of corn and wine-filled grapes.
The deep placid lake like the steady mind of a sage.
Mystical sound of the playful encroaching waves.
The sun that makes a bed of crimson red to rest,
and Hands that write blinding forks of light.

Cosmic Travelers

All hitched a ride on a vast merry-go-round
since the first-born morn,
when a golden splendor flooded sea and land.
Each day closes its lamp, sinks under the horizon
for stars to lift the night with celestial songs.

Hurtling faster than a screaming jet
while under a canopy of banana leaves we rest,
the level on a sturdy beam is set,
a thread goes through the eye of a needle,
and pilgrims lumbered to the top of the steeple.

A motion constant like a sweet, dreamy cruise.
To feel this merry-go-round never moves.
Then the rush of day and night,
bite of winter's blast, crisp air of spring at last—
we are cosmic travelers in time and space.

That Dreaded Classroom

A child snatched from the arms of Mother Nature.
My eyes strained in that dreaded classroom.
My back lumbered as if from long labor.
The hours boring and tiresome,
but saved by the sweet sound of the last bell,
as I ran to behold the red-breasted robin
sang to the river that rushed with a swell.

I felt like a falcon with its wings sheared.
I longed for the grassy fields, the open air—
sink my little feet in soft mud,
and watch flowers unfurled from their buds.
The crowded classroom held no charms.
I cried to roam the woods and fields I belong—
play, sing, and dance in sun and rains.

Regimented and drilled,
my mind a bucket to fill,
and then to unload and load again.
A mindless conformity—the fields
of childhood cramped in an aisle of monotony.
And never a glow in my heart,
as when the sun made a band of gold for the sea.

Far-Off Places

Enough of this contented rest—
these familiar streets and thoroughfares.
My mind roams to far-off places.
My eyes would rather be there:

to plumb the depths of the Grand Canyon
soar like a falcon over forests of the Amazon
stroll along banks of the sacred Ganges
watch mighty elephants dance in the Serengeti

to gaze in wonder at the Northern Lights
sprawling cities with ten thousand delights
to stare at Niagara tumbling to a sweet misty rebound
and Mount Fuji framed by delicate cherry blossoms

to behold geometry rising in the Giza Plateau
the Great Pyramids that hold the secrets of Egypt
to stare at love revealed in artistic beauty
the Taj Mahal celebrating life in gleaming marble.

Like the Space Unscathed

I am not this frail human
mocked by disease and time.
Who feels for the way
when the lights go out.

I am not this fragile being
who trembles when the fever is high,
and for a lost love,
like a child bitterly cries.

I am not this wanderer
who settles for dust when the stars beckon.
Who sits by the shore and laments
while the sea swells in blissful content.

I am not this pot of clay,
this tattered coat I carry.
I have within such grit and will,
can cut through walls of granite and steel.

I am the immortal self
sheathed in a mortal coil—
when extinguished, I remain inviolate,
like the space unscathed when the pot is broken.

No race, no lineage can stamp on my being.

Like the wind I ride unseen,
and like the oceans—
I reach every shore, every clime.

Rising from the Ashes

Twisting and swaying in its macabre dance.
the fire stretched out its tongues.
Sent a red glowing sunset in the sky,
and with ghoulish shouts
leaped and devoured the forest.
In its ghastly trail fields of blackened bodies,
charred bones, and an eerie silence of blighted souls—
snatched before their dreams were told.

But long-slept seeds heard their cries.
Woke up and ploughed through the ashes
like an elephant pushing through bushes.
And ere long a miracle wrought —
from a grisly jungle of charred stumps
a lively forest slowly stretched its limbs,
gazed at the distant cloud drenched mountains,
and smiled and whispered softly in the winds.

A Gentle Whisper

I asked that unruffled calm of nature
if it is mute to our entreaties and cries.
Then a gentle whisper I heard:
"Remember when I stood by your side,
and wiped the tears from your eyes.
When your days were lonesome,
and your nights were restless,
and I lifted you from the valley of darkness
to feast from the finest of my fields and orchards.
And even when you turned from my light
you were never out of my sight,
and I waited and waited and waited
until you hitched unto me a ride—
when you never felt so free,
like a falcon gliding over the sea."

Dawn

Wake up!
No dream holds more beauty.
Behold the dawn!
A palette of mystical colors
nature paints over plains, hills, and seas,
and beckons the day to rise
with rhythms of life and joy.

The world stirs from its slumber.
Cares little for this moving hour.
And in the slumber of hurried wakefulness
the celestial dawn quietly vanishes.
But no sweeter charm, no sweeter calm,
gaze of intent on the dawn—
the stuff of meditation and songs.

What better scenes to flood these eyes.
This loving embrace of day and night.
This canvas of wonder across the sky.
Tints of purple, pink, orange, and crimson—
this playful battle of colors,
and ever-changing robes of Mother Earth,
as she softly plays on unearthly strings.

Along the sacred river
a boatman bursts into songs of rapture.

A farmer trekking to his fields
lifts his hands in prayer.
And a poet searches his heart
for a glittering frame
to enclose a magical wonder—the glory of dawn.

A Ship

There's a ship out there.
She rides the sea with such ease.
The waves climb to break her bones.
She shows a steady bow and stern.
Bestrides the danger with such composure.
An unyielding power in her keel
to reveal such nerves of steel.

A rare courage and defiance
to a sea angry, restless, and stubborn.
No blast from wind or wave,
no surging current in the dark depths,
to dampen her spirit, delay her course set.

On the sea of life straddled before our eyes,
like that ship we must ride.
There're bound to be storms,
billows, whirlpools, and currents swift and strong,
but we must sail on.

A Smile & A Song

A smile and a song:
to open the windows at dawn,
greet the resplendent sun,
and the world.
Take in the scent of flowers,
hasten the day along,
and reveal a heart that belongs to nature
that smiles and sings day long.

Two lovers meet besides a pond.
A smile greets a song.
They kiss and hold hands,
and no place for what ails the world
in their eager tight embrace.

The power in a smile and a song.
Can blunt the edge of a storm.
And life's burdens much lighter—
smiling at the bending path further,
humming a tune with fervor.

Waiting for Spring

As a person fallen on hard times
waits for the stars to shine.
As the moon on the wane
longs for its fullness again.
So, I watch and wait,
like a bird calling for a mate,
for spring to show its face.

Long for that carpet of green
soft, tender, and moist,
open bed to rest and rejoice,
mend a broken heart
or simply gaze at the clouds,
and invigorate body
with that primal vitality.

Long for white, pink, and red buds—
eyes ready to open.
Tender leaves shooting out of limbs,
fragrant blossoms and burst of azaleas—
fanfare of beauty, splendor, and color.

Long for sparrows and wrens
to serenade on branches again.
Sounds of bees, frogs, and insects,
carnival and revelry on the march.

Sweet music: a band playing on
when the crowds have gone.
Rousing beats for a weary mind and heart,
long bitter winter wrought.

Long for the outdoors alone
to gaze at the sky.
Inhale mint-laden spring air,
rain and soil, grasses, twigs, and leaves—
intoxicating perfume for mind and body,
no bottled scent can carry.

But most of all
long for the laughter of children,
smiles on faces of men and women.
A song, a glow from deep within.
Human warmth from slumber awakened,
to mingle with scent of chrysanthemums.

A Song, A Poem, A Dance

I listen to the sermons, recitations, and exhortations,
the honey dripping tongues of humans.
But a far greater peace to me:
beholding the tranquil deep blue sea,
gazing at a mulberry tree,
a flock of flamingoes flying high,
the beauty of a tiger moth butterfly,
and a constellation of stars in the night's sky.
In them I discern
what abides eternally within,
what inspires a poem, a song,
and moves the human heart to dance.

Heart, Flesh & Bones

The heart of the willow bleeds
for wounded limbs.
The fingers move the pen,
but it's the heart of the poet that writes.
The world to hear his exultations and cries.
A builder sees a foundation strong,
a mighty tower on its head to rest—
not the color of the sand and stones
that comprise its flesh and bones.

A refreshing drink in the heart of a coconut,
guarded by layers of fibers thick.
In the heart of the sea
the sunken depths of utter stillness,
though its surface thronged with fearful billows.
And the infant cries
to be close to its mother's heart—
feels not the pangs of her tattered coat,
nor the smooth touch of her silken dress.

That's the Place

Where laughter of children resound.
Game of cards with friends around.
Aroma of corn bread, muffins
of raspberry, vanilla ice cream, a guitar
on table, a hammock under the tree.
Murmur of waves and buzz of bees,
and when it's supper—
time for hearts to gather.

Where the stars in the Milky Way
not shrouded by curtains of dismay.
Rustle of the wind, songs of the robin
not ruffled by discordant notes within.
A splendid mansion on the hill,
or a simple dwelling on bamboo stilts—
that's the place my heart craves
to the end of my days.

The Mirror

Beaming smiles,
and the mirror shines no brighter.
Wretched angry distorted faces,
and the mirror does not crack.
The mirror unaffected by what it discloses.
When we wipe every dust, every cloud from its face,
reveals every line, every feature of vigor or decline,
and a hint perhaps of how we look deep inside.

The mirror never partakes of our sorrows and joys,
though we stare at it and laugh and cry.
When we see a bloodied head,
it's not that the mirror has suffered a fall.
When we see a jolly face,
it's not a mirror of another make.
And when there's a deep gash on the face—
don't blame the fair mirror,
but the unsteady hand that held the blade.

That's When

A thousand reasons to detain,
that's when the journey to begin.
A thousand reasons to be complacent,
that's when to lift muscles and hurl the javelin,
and flow like restless streams from the mountain.

A thousand reasons to be sad,
that's when to smile with a song in the heart.
A thousand reasons to fear,
that's when to ride the waves, unfurl the sails.
A thousand bells of temptations ring,
that's when like a mountain never to yield.

A thousand sighs, a thousand cries,
a thousand agonies, a thousand wounds,
that's when to rush and ease the pain.
And when a thousand lights go out,
that's when a little lamp will sing aloud.

If We Could

The ripened years—
no time to bid the days away,
a foreboding of those to come.
But:
if we could in heart be young
more kisses and hugs,
more songs to sing,
more tunes to hum,
dancing to the new tempo and rhythm.

More woods and fields to roam.
More rocks to climb,
more lands to see and explore,
more dreams to chase,
with less speed and haste.

If we could have the strength:
to bend and pluck the weeds,
trim hedges, break rotten fences,
stroll the beaten pathways—
a new barber in town to greet.

More miles to cross
to warm the heart
with beads of sweat on forehead.
A new flower, a new scent along the path,

a beautiful sunset,
then snuggle like a child in bed.

If we could feel the thrill of a symphony.
Wander in museums, galleries, and libraries.
A new game, a new language to learn,
forge a bond with minds active and strong.

If we could take in the news of the day.
Lift our hands to faces wrinkled in despair.
Sit by the shore with a friend,
memories of years long spent—
refreshed in the silent waves of the moment.

If we could be whole in mind and body.
Bear the pains in back and joints.
Recall the names of people and places.
Put up a backyard shed,
climb the stairs,
button shirts, pull up trousers,
tighten laces on boots,
mingle with the crowd,
and bear the stench and noise.

If we could be like a lark
contented in mind and heart,
and as the sunflower seeks the sun
with every beat of the heart
yearn for the Sweet Lord.
No earthly desires, no feverish thirst
to muffle the drums as the sun goes down,

but like clouds soaring high,
or a released, long-suffering caged bird—
flapping its wings as it quickly flies.

Oh! Little Canary

No court sat in hushed silence.
No jury pronounced the sentence.
Yet imprisoned for life in a tiny cage,
how cruel a fate
Oh! little canary,
and for what ill deed—
to sing in the woods melodies sweet,
kiss the clouds, and roam over waters deep.

If such a fate to any human,
shouts of outrage over the land.
But the world in silence conspires
to mock your wings and colorful feathers.
Every piece of wood, every wire fashioned
a cage to suppress a spirit
that once rode over the cliffs,
and sat on the treetops: its mate to serenade.

About the Author

Haimnauth Ramkirath was born in the Republic of Guyana, perched at the very tip of South America. He grew up in a small village of rustic beauty and charm, where the rhythms of life were predictable and simple. As a child, he immersed himself completely in the fascination and beauty of the natural world. This love for nature is still one of the abiding joys of his life and is reflected in many of his poems.

Haimnauth was a teacher for almost ten years at the secondary school level in Guyana. He came to the USA in 1991. He is a professional Accountant who has worked his way up to the Controller level. He lives in Bayonne, NJ with his wife, Radhika, his daughter, Tamala, and son, Akash.

Haimnauth Ramkirath is an ardent practitioner of meditation, yoga, and the ancient science of Ayurvedic healing. He is a motivational speaker, and a vigorous campaigner for social justice and equality.

www.ingramcontent.com/pod-product-compliance
Lightning Source LLC
Chambersburg PA
CBHW030909080526
44589CB00010B/221